Janet Adams

MORE PRACTICAL TOPICS FOR THE EARLY YEARS

Published by:
"TOPICAL RESOURCES"

More Practical Topics for the Early Years by Janet Adams

INTRODUCTION

2nd book by Janet Adams.

A follow up to Practical Topics for the Early Years.

These books are designed to assist adults working with children in playgroups, nurseries and reception classes.

This book covers the themes counting, animals and shapes. The first book looked at colour, opposites, weather and seasons and ourselves.

Each activity has a basic concept to explore, something to make, photocopiable activity, a rhyme to learn, suggestions for discussion and a follow up activity.

Illustrated by Paul Sealey.

Printed in Great Britain for "Topical Resources" publishers of Educational Materials, PO Box 329, Broughton, Preston PR3 5LT, Telephone 01772 863158 by T Snape and Co. Ltd., Bolton's Court, Preston, Lancs.

Typeset by White Cross Business Support Service, White Cross, Lancaster.

First published April 1995.

ISBN 1-872977-20-0.

CONTENTS

COUNTING

ANIMALS

SHAPE

COUNTING

ONE and TWO

Make: **A Face**

Face outline as shown opposite.
Potatoes and carrots.
Paint - pink, blue, red.

1. Photocopy or trace the outline as shown opposite. One for each child.

2. Using quite a small potato, slice a shape suitable for an ear and a mouth.

3. Using a carrot, slice off pieces for a nose and eyes.

4. Prepare the paints. Pour small amounts onto some margarine tub lids to avoid unnecessary waste and spillage.

5. Use the vegetable shapes as printing blocks and print the appropriate number of features, in the correct colours onto the face.

Rhyme:

2 little eyes to look around,
2 little ears to hear each sound.
1 little nose to smell what's sweet,
And 1 little mouth that likes to eat.

Activity: Using a fine pen, draw a face on the forefinger of each child's hands. Use the fingers as puppets to say:

Two fat gentlemen met in a lane
Bowed most politely, bowed oncc again
How do you do? How do you do?
And how do you do again?

Talk about: The numbers 1 and 2 associated with our bodies.

front

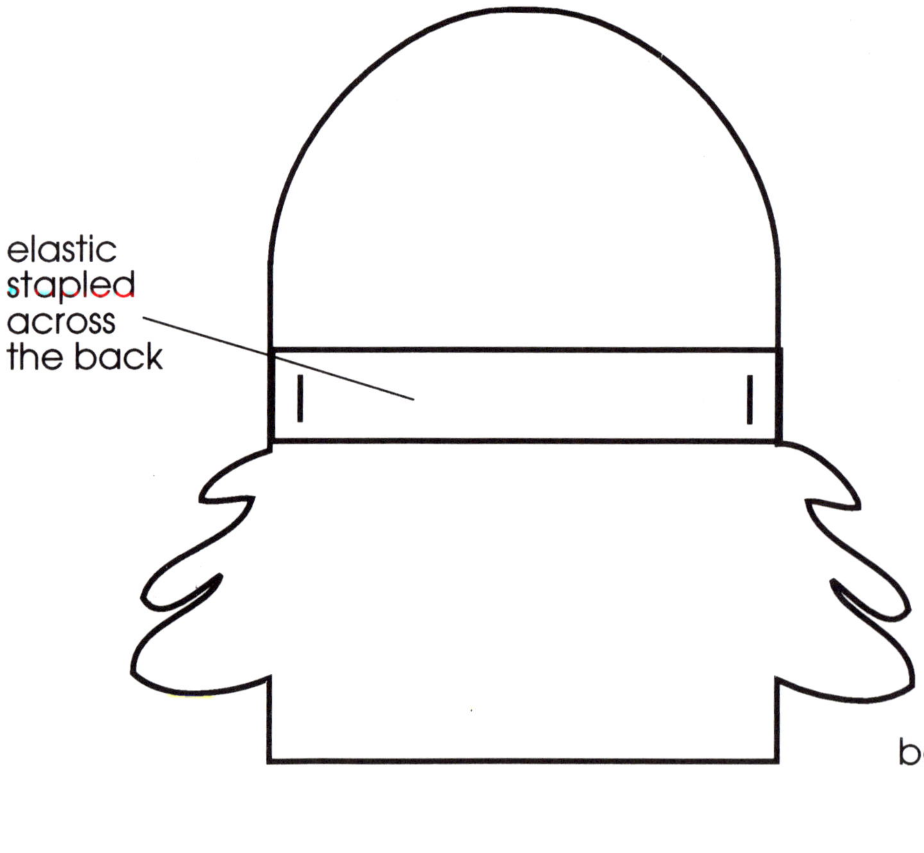

back

TWO

Make: **2 little dicky birds**

Yellow card
Black crayon/felt pen
Elastic
Stapler
Orange card/gummed paper cut into 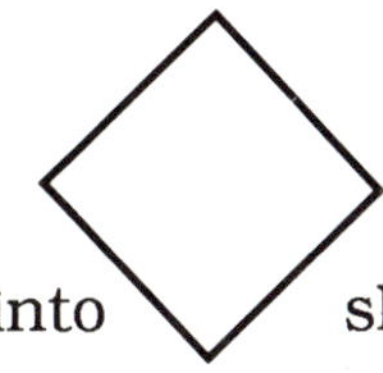 shapes
Scissors
Pencil

1. Make templates as shown opposite.

2. Each child draws round a template and cuts out 2 birds from yellow card.

3. Draw 2 eyes on each bird with black crayon/felt pen and stick on a beak from orange card.

4. Staple a piece of elastic around the back of each bird from one side to the other so it goes around the child's hand.

5. Put a bird on each hand ready to say the rhyme.

Rhyme:

2 little dicky birds, sitting on a wall,
One named Peter, one named Paul.
Fly away Peter, fly away Paul;
Come back Peter, come back Paul.

Activity: Make sets of 2's. On a large piece of paper draw round shapes in 2's eg 2 circles, 2 triangles, 2 wheels or cut out pictures from magazines and catalogues eg 2 wheels, 2 cars, 2 books, 2 shoes. Draw a circle around each pair and decorate the page by filling in the spaces with number 2's.

Talk about:

Things around us that are in 2's.
Pairs of things eg socks, shoes etc.
Bicycle - cycle with 2 wheels.

Baa Baa Black Sheep
Have you any wool?

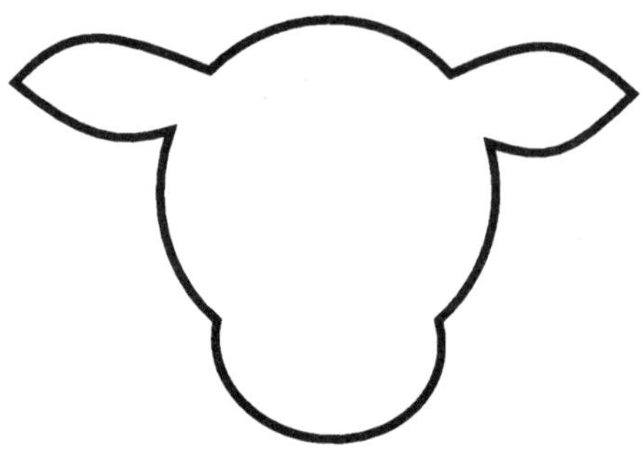

THREE

Make: **<u>Baa baa black sheep</u>**

Newsprint paper
Brown paper (old envelopes/wrapping paper)
Black animal bedding (from a pet shop) or
Black chopped up wool
Glue
Black paper
Pencils
Scissors

1. Each child needs a piece of paper wide enough for the completed picture, as shown opposite, to fit onto. (A3 cut into 3)

2. Prepare templates of a bag. Each child needs 3 bags cut out of brown paper.

3. Stick on to the picture a 'blob' of animal bedding (e.g. hamster type bedding) to make the sheeps body. Either put a smaller blob for the sheep's head or cut out heads from black paper (probably better cut out by an adult as they are quite small. Use template of sheep's head).

4. Stick 3 bags onto the paper, draw some string around the top of each and write the numbers on as shown.

5. Write the first line of the rhyme at the top of the paper.

Rhyme:

Baa, baa black sheep, have you any wool?
Yes sir, yes sir, 3 bags full.
One for the master, one for the dame,
And one for the little boy who lives down the lane.

Activity: Using Clay (the sort that doesn't need firing), plasticine or play dough, make 3 mice. Shape the nose and ears with the fingers. Use a pencil point to make the eyes. Make a hole in the rear of each mouse and insert a small length of string for the tail. Mould the clay around the string to secure it:- 3 blind mice.

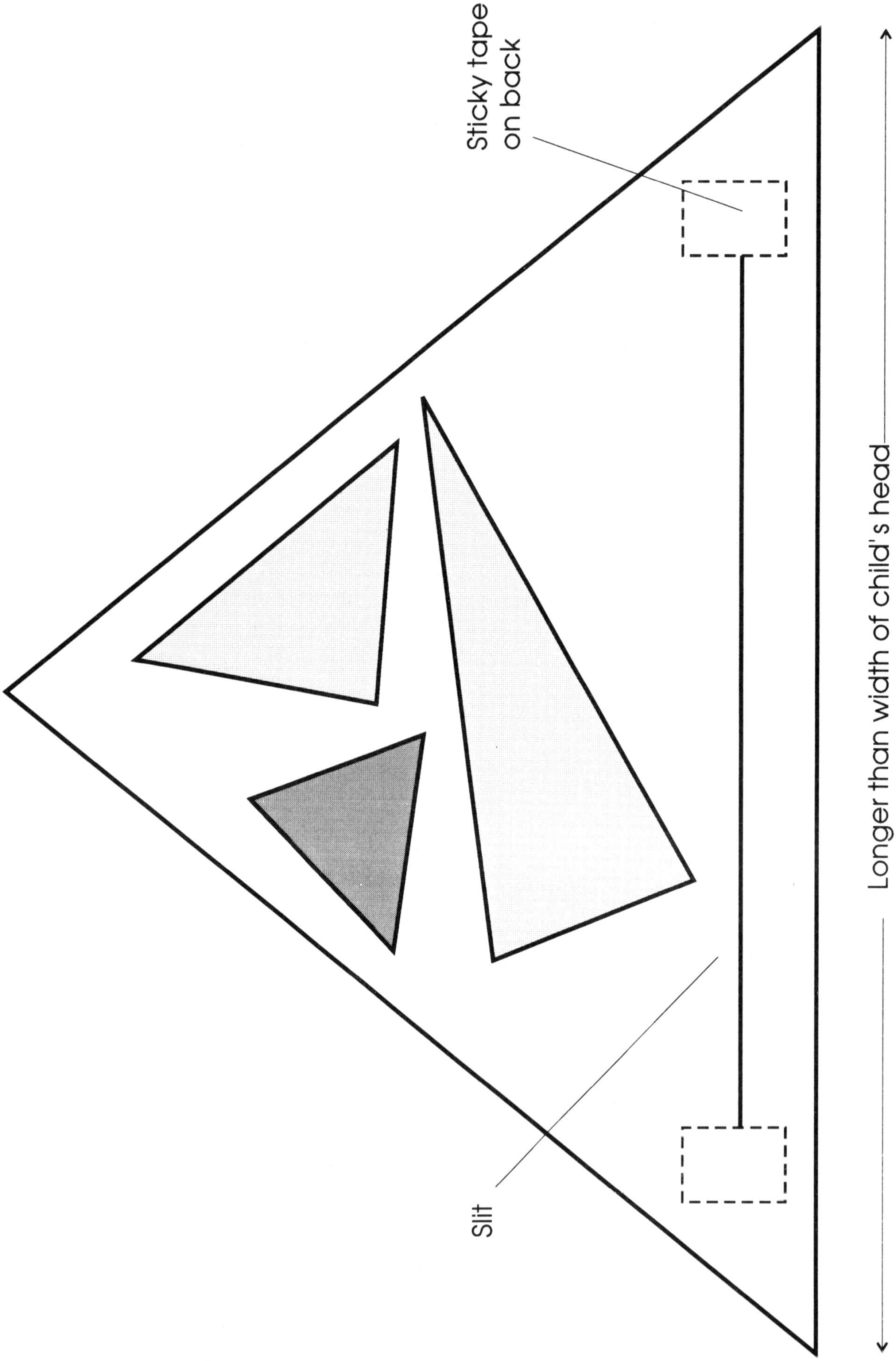
Sticky tape
on back
Slit
Longer than width of child's head

THREE

Make: **A 3 cornered hat**

Large sheets coloured activity paper
Gummed triangles or triangular sponges and paints or crayons
Scissors
Sticky tape

1. Cut out a large triangle of coloured activity paper ensuring that the base of the triangle is longer than the width of the child's head. The two other sides of the triangle should be the same length as each other.

2. Fold the triangle in half and cut carefully, as shown, making a slit for the hat to fit onto the child's head. When it is the correct size fix sticky tape at the ends of the cut to prevent the paper from tearing.

3. On the front of the hat stick 3 coloured triangles or print 3 triangles or draw and colour 3 triangles.

Rhyme: My hat it has 3 corners,
3 corners has my hat.
And had it not 3 corners,
It would not be my hat.

Activity: Make a bear mask modifying the pattern of a rabbit mask on page 38 by changing the shape of the ears. Colour the mask brown and put fur fabric on the ears. Use brown face paint on the child's nose.

Talk about: The story of Goldilocks and the 3 bears, with particular emphasis on the number 3. Have pictures or real examples or doll's house examples of 3 bowls, 3 chairs, 3 beds and 3 different sized teddy bears.
Talk about size.
Dramatize the story in groups.

4 currant buns in a baker's shop

1 2 3 4

FOUR

Make: **4 Currant buns**

A3 activity paper
White chalk/crayon
Black crayon
Brown paper
Stapler

1. For each child, fold a piece of A3 in half lengthways. Open out again then fold up to the crease and then over to make a pocket. Staple at the ends (see diagram). Along the pocket write 1 2 3 4.

2. Prepare templates of the currant bun or photocopy 4 onto card for children to cut out and colour.

3. Each child cuts out 4 buns from brown paper. Using white chalk/crayon colour some icing on the top of each bun and draw some currants with black crayon.

4. Place the 4 buns into the pocket.

Rhyme:

4 currant buns in a baker's shop,
Round and fat with sugar on the top.
Along came a boy with a penny one day,
Bought a currant bun and took it away.
(Remove a bun from the pocket for each verse
until there are none left).

Activity:

Make 4 sandwiches. Use 2 slices of bread sandwiched together with margarine and jam. Use biscuit cutter(s) and cut out 4 small sandwiches. If not to be eaten there and then, take home on a cardboard plate covered with film. (There are cardboard plates available with numbers printed on them)

Find on page 20 a sheet the children can fill in and take home about this activity.

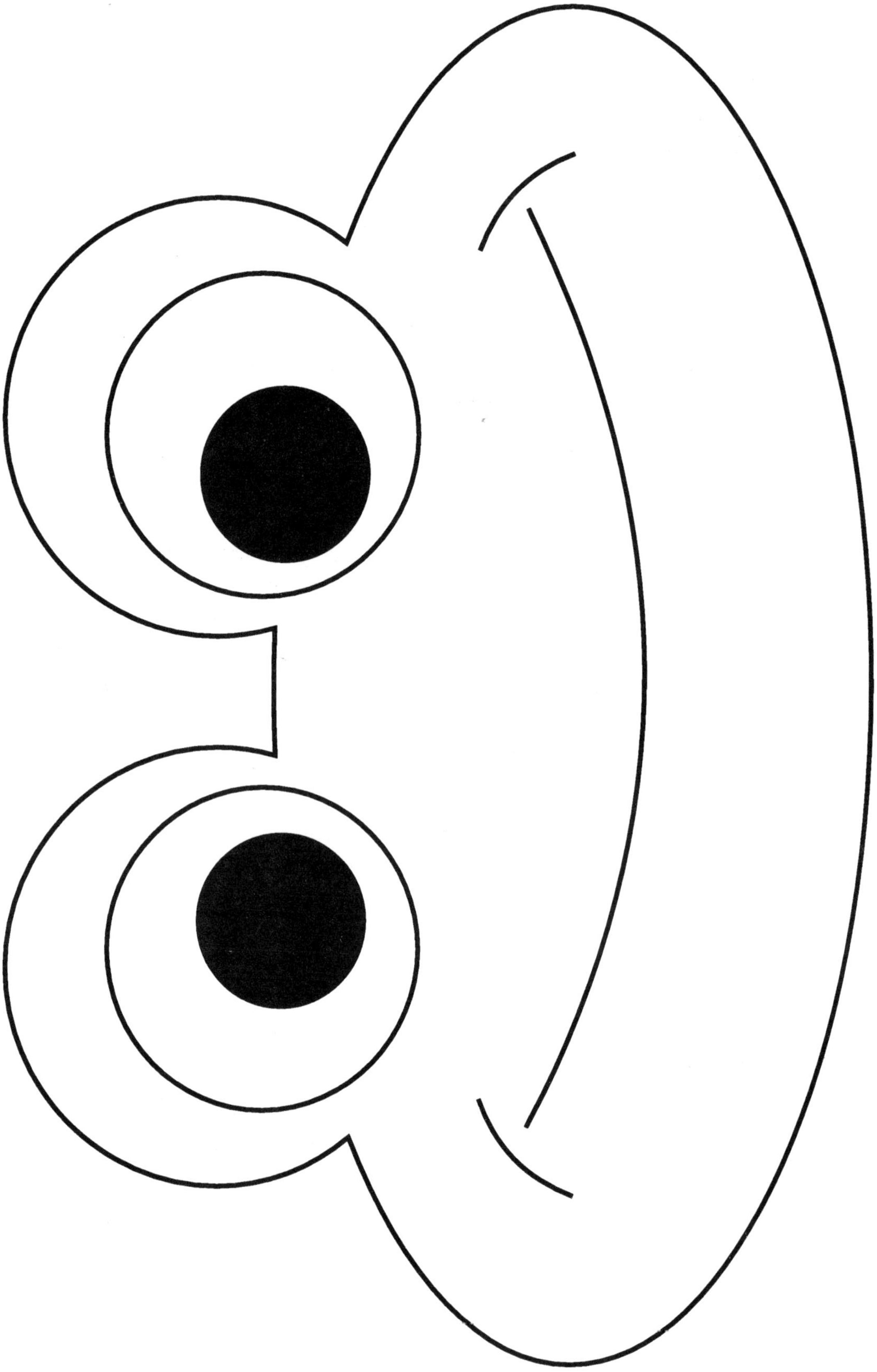

FOUR

Make: **A little froggy mask**

Green luminous card
Black paper
White paper
Black crayon
Strips of dark coloured card
Scissors
Stapler

1. Prepare templates of the frog's head and eye pieces.

2. Each child cuts out a frog's head, 2 large white circles and 2 smaller black circles.

3. Stick the eyes onto the right part of the face. Draw mouth onto the face with a black crayon (or this could be drawn lightly in dots, then children can join up the dots with the crayon).

4. The mask is to be worn across the forehead and not in front of the eyes, so fix a piece of card across the back to reach round the child's head. Staple the card onto the sides of the mask.

   Now act out the rhyme in groups of 4.

Rhyme:

4 little froggies sitting on a well,
One looked up and down he fell.
Froggies jumped high, froggies jumped low,
3 little froggies dancing to and fro.

Activity: Find 4 kinds of pasta which can be threaded onto wool. Let each child thread 4 pieces of the 4 kinds of pasta onto the wool counting in sets of 4.

Talk about: Sets of 4's - wheels on vehicles, legs on animals. 4 legs on chairs / tables etc. What happens if a leg was taken away?

1
2
3
4
5

FIVE

Make: **5 apples on a tree**

Card
Green activity paper
Brown paper (wrapping paper)
Red paper
Pencils
Scissors
Glue

1. Using the card make templates of the 5 apples. (see opposite page)

2. Make a tree shape with green paper, as shown, big enough for all 5 apples to fit onto. The tree on the opposite page is to show how to display this.

3. Stick a trunk underneath using the brown paper.

4. Draw round each apple template onto the tree.

5. Draw round each apple template onto the red paper and cut each one out.

6. Match each red apple with one on the tree and stick down.

7. Write the numbers one to five on or by each apple.

Rhyme:

5 red apples growing on a tree,
One fell off and rolled to me.
4 red apples .... 3 red apples ... 2 red apples
1 red apple growing on a tree,
It fell off and rolled to me.
5 red apples rolled to me,
I'll take them home and eat them for tea! (J.A.)

Activity: Collect 5 large dried leaves and stick them onto a drawn tree. Colour the trunk by rubbing over a piece of bark.

Talk about: Count the fingers on one hand. Think about all the number rhymes which have the numbers 1 - 5.
eg 5 little ducks, 5 little speckled frogs.

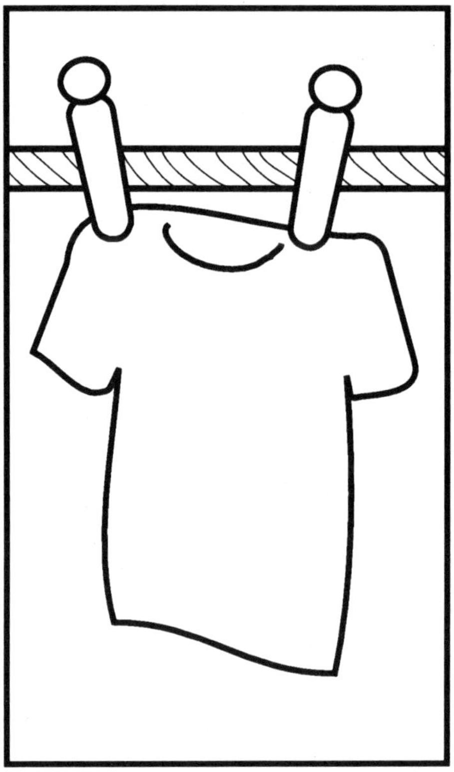
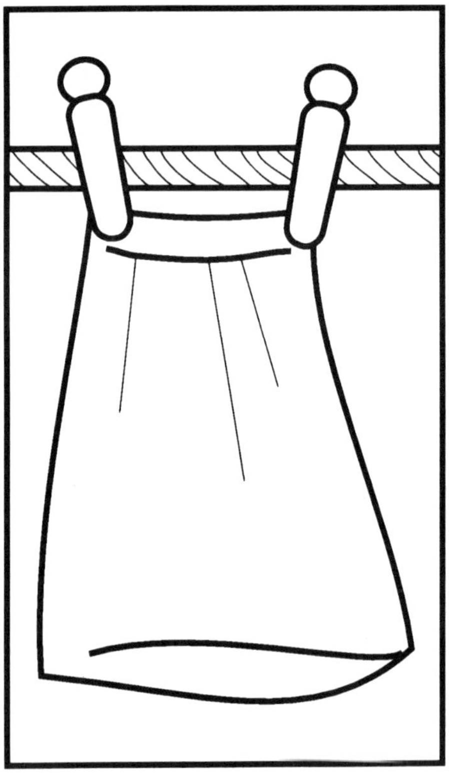
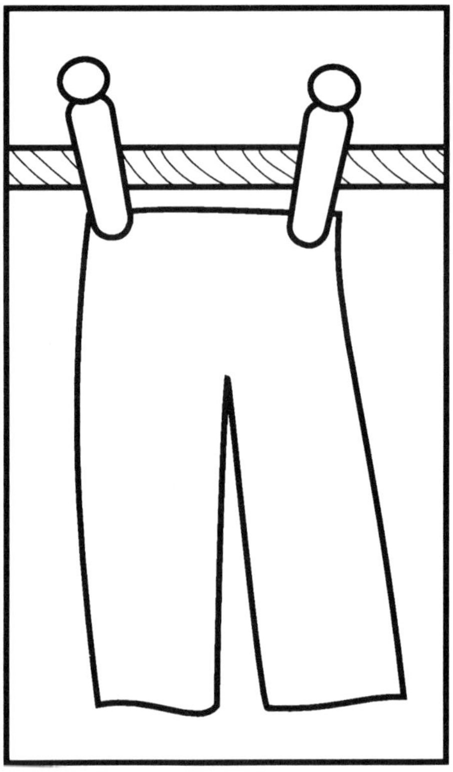

FIVE

Make: <u>**Shirts on a washing line**</u>

Card
A4 paper - coloured or white
Felt pens
Scissors
Pencils

1. Copy the shape of the shirt on a line and make a template out of card.

2. Fold a piece of A4 paper in half lengthways and cut into 2 pieces.

3. Using one piece per child fold the paper into 5 concertina style.

4. Place template onto folded paper and draw round it.

5. Cut out carefully and using felt pens colour the clothes, pegs and washing line.

Rhyme:

5 shirts blowing on a line so high,
Unpeg one because it's dry!
4 shirts ..... etc JA

The children can make up more verses with, for example socks, vests, skirts, shorts etc. Until all the washing is dry.

Activity:

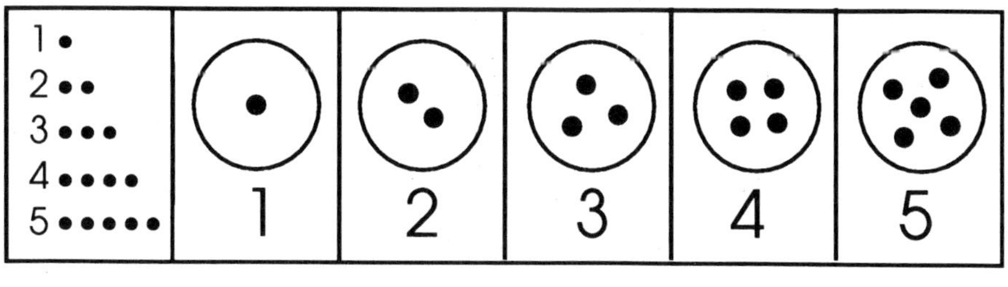

Using a strip of paper fold into 6, concertina style. Make the first Section the front cover and write on it as shown. On the rest draw a circle and the child has to put the correct number of adhesive spots in each circle 1 to 5. Practise writing the numbers at the bottom of each page.

Today we made ☐ sandwiches

We used ☐ slices of bread,

a knife,

a spoon,

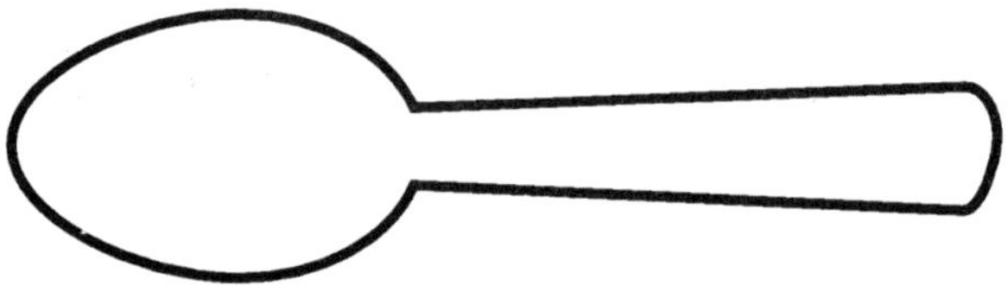

some jam,

some margarine,

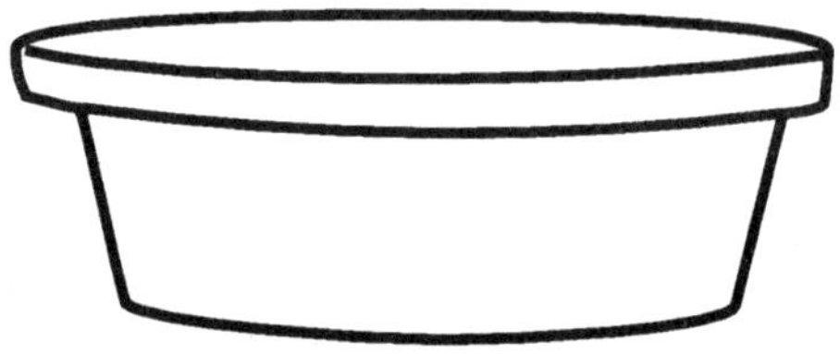

and ☐ biscuit cutters.

ANIMALS

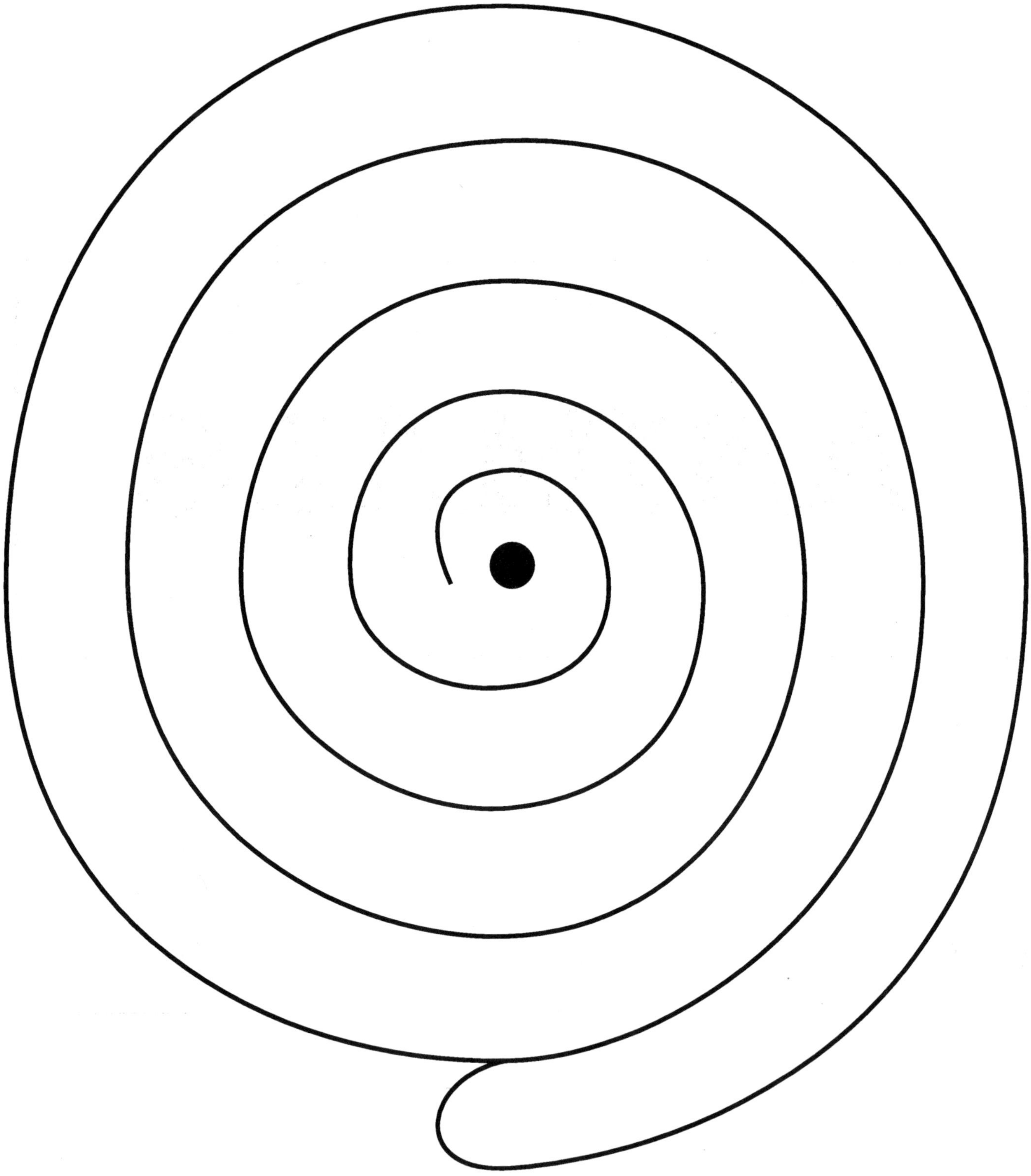

SNAKE

Make: **A Mobile**

White A4 paper
Multicoloured crayons/double headed felt pens
Needle and thread
Scissors

1. Make a copy of the snake opposite for each child.

2. Before cutting out, make patterns on the snake using the crayons or felt pens, the more colourful the better.

3. On the reverse side draw the outline of the snake and let the child colour on the back, so that the snake is coloured on both sides.

4. Starting at the tip of the tail, carefully cut out the snake.

5. Thread a length of cotton through the snake's head.

6. Hang from the ceiling or a tree collage or fix onto a stick/straw to use as a puppet.

Rhyme:

Sammy is a snake,
He slides along the ground,
He is so very quiet,
He hardly makes a sound.

Sammy is a snake,
When curled up is quite small,
But when he gets cross and angry,
He rises up so tall.

JA

Activity: Make a snake by threading cotton reels together. Stick a card face at the end.

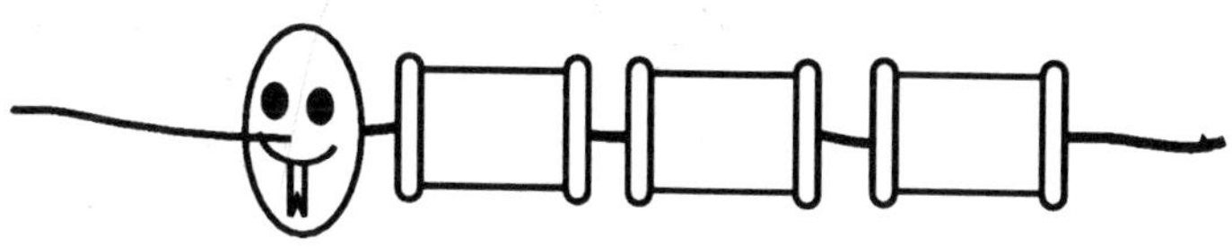

Talk about: The noise a snake makes. How does a snake move? Move our arms and bodies like snakes. Words that make us think about snakes, eg slippery, shiny, squiggling, hissing etc. Patterns and colours of snake skins.

ELEPHANT

Make: **An elephant with a rug on its back**

Card for template
Grey card
White wax crayon
Black felt pen
Coloured binca
Embroidery silks — Scissors
Needles (not sharp) — Glue

1. Make a template of the elephant from the illustration opposite.

2. Cut out 2 elephants from the grey card.

3. Stick the elephants together by the head, back, tail and trunk to the level of the tops of the legs.

4. Colour the tusks white, separate them out and open the legs so that the elephant can stand up.

5. Draw the eyes and feet with black felt pen

6. Cut out the binca 16 x 9 cm per elephant.

7. Sew round the binca with coloured threads and stitches (according to the ability of the child).

8. When completed, the mat may need to be pressed and folded along the middle.

9. Lie the mat across the elephant's back.

10. Fix on with a staple or stitch.

Rhyme:

An elephant went out to play,
Upon a piece of string one day.
He thought it such tremendous fun,
He called for another elephant to come.
Two elephants ... etc.

Activity: Make a finger puppet using this pattern from grey card to illustrate the above rhyme.

Talk about:

What is special about an elephant?
What does he use his trunk for?
Where do elephants live?
How do they move? Are they fast/slow animals?
Big/little, heavy/light etc
What are baby elephants called?

LION

Make: **A mask**

Yellow and orange activity paper
Black felt pen
Glue
Elastic and needle
Scissors
Card for templates

1. Make templates of the mane or by drawing a circle radius 10 cm and another circle radius 8.5 cm. Make a template of the lion's face.

2. Using the 10 cm circle template cut out a circle using yellow paper and an 8.5 cm circle from the orange paper.

3. Snip round the edges of the circles to make a fringe.

4. Stick the mane pieces on top of each other.

5. Cut the face out of yellow paper and draw on the nose and mouth. Stick onto the mane.

6. Cut through the three layers to make the eyes (probably too difficult for small children)

7. Fix elastic at the sides to make a mask. Another layer of mane could be added to make the lion look larger.

Rhyme:

Who's the King of the Jungle?
The Lion said, "It's me!
And if you don't behave yourselves,
I'll eat you for my tea!"

Activity: Make a pair of binoculars for looking at the animals in the jungle. Cover 2 card tubes with paper eg children's wallpaper/ wrapping paper. Glue the 2 tubes together, secure with a staple if necessary. Thread string through the sides.

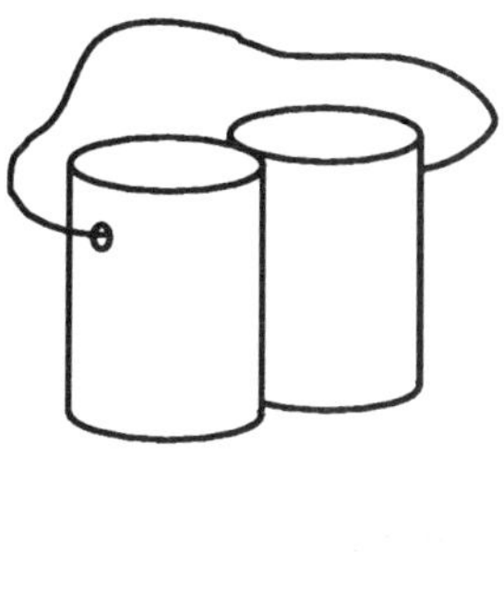

MONKEY

Make: **A Collage**

Brown animal bedding and/or brown material
Brown felt
Yellow felt
Glue
Scissors
Fine black felt pen

1. Make a copy of the monkey for each child.
2. Stick animal bedding onto the body but not on the face.
3. Stick brown felt onto the face either in bits or as a cut out shape.
4. When the felt is dry draw on eyes, nose and mouth.
5. Stick felt onto the ears, hands and feet.
6. Cut out the banana from yellow felt and stick onto the monkey's hand.
7. When dry the monkeys could be cut out and stuck onto a jungle collage.

Rhyme:

5 little monkeys jumping on the bed,
One fell off and bumped his head.
Mummy called the doctor,
And the doctor said:
"No more monkeys jumping on the bed!"
4 little monkeys .... etc 3 ... 2 ...
One little monkey jumping on the bed,
He fell off and bumped his head.
Mummy called the doctor,
And the doctor said:
"Put those monkeys straight to bed!"

Activity: Make a camera for taking photographs of all the animals. Use a small teabag box or something similar. Stick a short piece of card tube to the front of the box. Fix a bottle top onto the top using a paper fastener. Thread wool/string through the sides.

Talk about: Different kinds of monkeys. How do monkeys move? How do they behave? Have you seen any monkeys? Where? What else did you see?

GIRAFFE

Make: **<u>A giraffe as tall as me</u>**

Paper roll (eg wallpaper/lining paper)
Yellow card
Corks (or something else suitable for printing with)
Yellow and brown paints
Scissors
Glue
Card for template

1. Using a long roll of paper cut out a giraffe's neck, body and legs.

2. Make a template of the giraffe's head then cut it out of yellow card.

3. By either cutting from the neck or the legs make the height of the giraffe the same as the child.

4. Print the body and the head with yellow and brown paints using corks.

5. Fix the head to the body when dry with glue or paper fasteners.

6. Photocopy the outline opposite again and make it into a certificate for each child with:-

    my giraffe and me
    are the same height.
    We are _____ cm tall
    __________ (date)

Rhyme:

1. Walking through the jungle what did I see?
   A tall giraffe peering at me, me, me!
2. Walking through ....
   A baby monkey laughing at me, me, me!
3. A fierce lion roaring.
4. An elephant trumpeting.
5. A slippery snake hissing.

Activity: Use the same outline opposite and transfer it onto yellow or brown card. Cut out the eyes. Colour with yellow or brown crayons. Fix elastic to sides to make a mask.

MOUSE

Make: **A field mouse in a field**

Shades of yellow and brown paint
Beige or black paper
Dried grasses with stems
Brown paper/felt
Scissors
Glue
Card for template

1. Carefully dip the grasses into the paint or paint the grasses with a paint brush then place each piece of grass onto the beige or black backing paper. Press down to make a print - place a clean piece of newspaper/kitchen paper on top of the grass whilst pressing to avoid getting too messy. Lift off the paper and then the grass carefully.

2. Repeat this with different shades of paint and different grasses to resemble a field. The effect is spoiled if it is too solid in colour.
   If the grasses are in a reasonable state after being used for printing, allow them to dry out then stick them onto the picture as well.

3. Make a template of a mouse.

4. Cut out a mouse (or mice) from brown paper/felt and stick onto the field.

Rhyme:

5 little mice sleeping in their nest,
One wakes up,
Two wake up,
And so do all the rest. JA

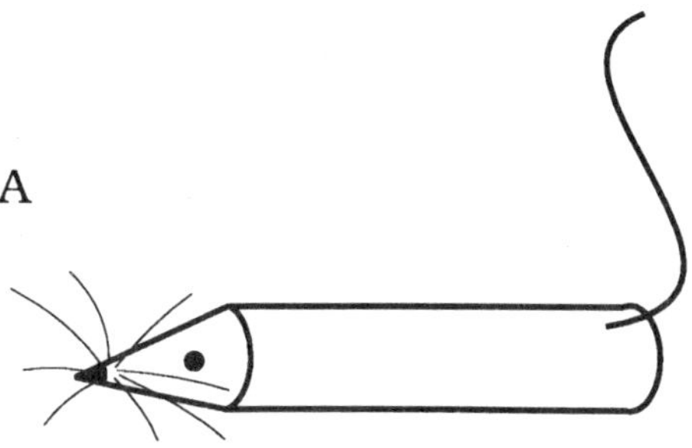

Activity: Make a toy mouse - Use a cardborad tube for the body, a cone of card fixed at one end to make a head. The whiskers and tail can be made from pipe cleaners and the eyes and nose drawn on with black felt pen.

Talk about: Has anyone got a pet mouse? Where do mice live?
Has anyone seen a mouse, other than a pet one?
Do you like mice? How do mice move?
Words to describe mice.

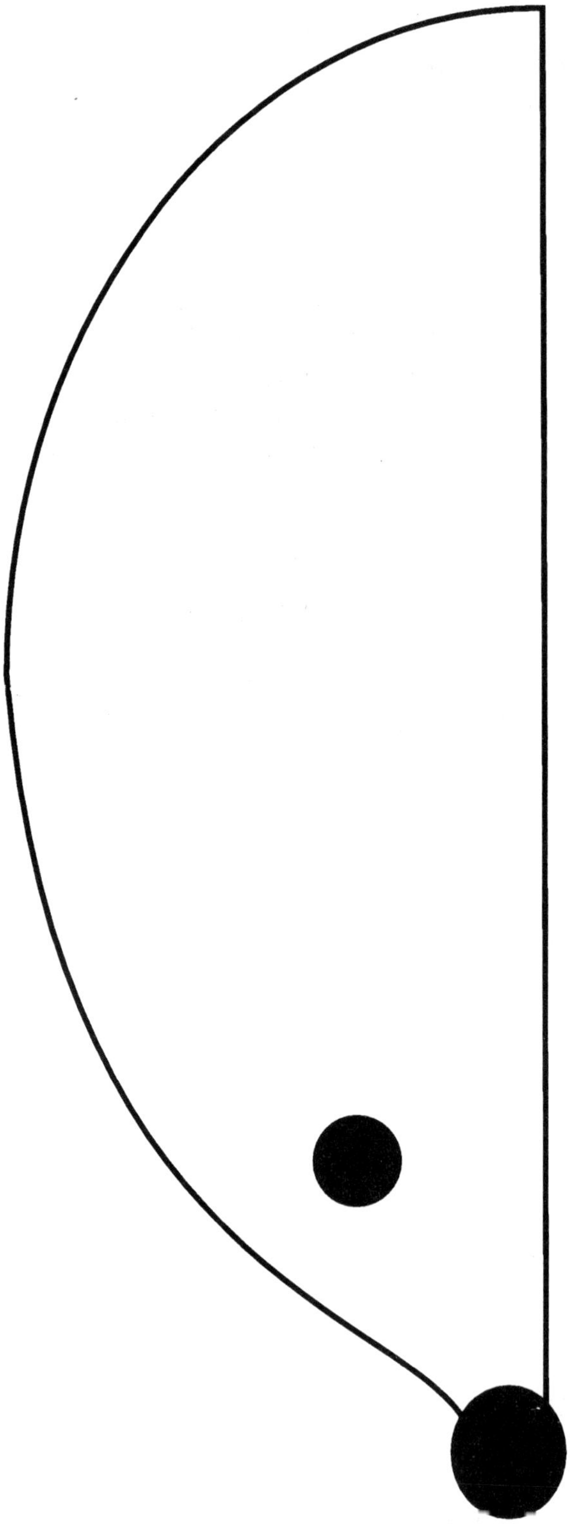

HEDGEHOG

Make: **A hedgehog**

Matchsticks or cut up straws
Green paper
Brown paper
Glue
Scissors
Card for template
Black felt pen

1. Make a template of the hedgehog and cut it out of brown paper.

2. Stick onto green background.

3. Cover the hedgehog with glue and stick on the matchsticks or straws to make the hedgehog look spikey,

4. Draw on an eye and a nose with felt pen.

Rhyme:

Little snuffling hedgehog,
Doesn't really care.
That his coat is brown and spikey,
With prickles and not hair!

He's really very happy,
Even though he's very small.
And when he's feeling tired
He rolls into a ball! JA

Activity: Make a hedgehog from clay (the sort that doesn't need firing), or playdough (which could be baked). Mould a piece of dough into a basic hedgehog shape, then use scissors to snip outwards to make spikes (or you can press in 1/2 matchsticks - but don't bake!)

Talk about:

Has anyone seen a hegehog?
Where do hedgehogs live?
What kind of coat does a hedgehog have?
How does a hedgehog move?
What does he eat?

Tommy's box

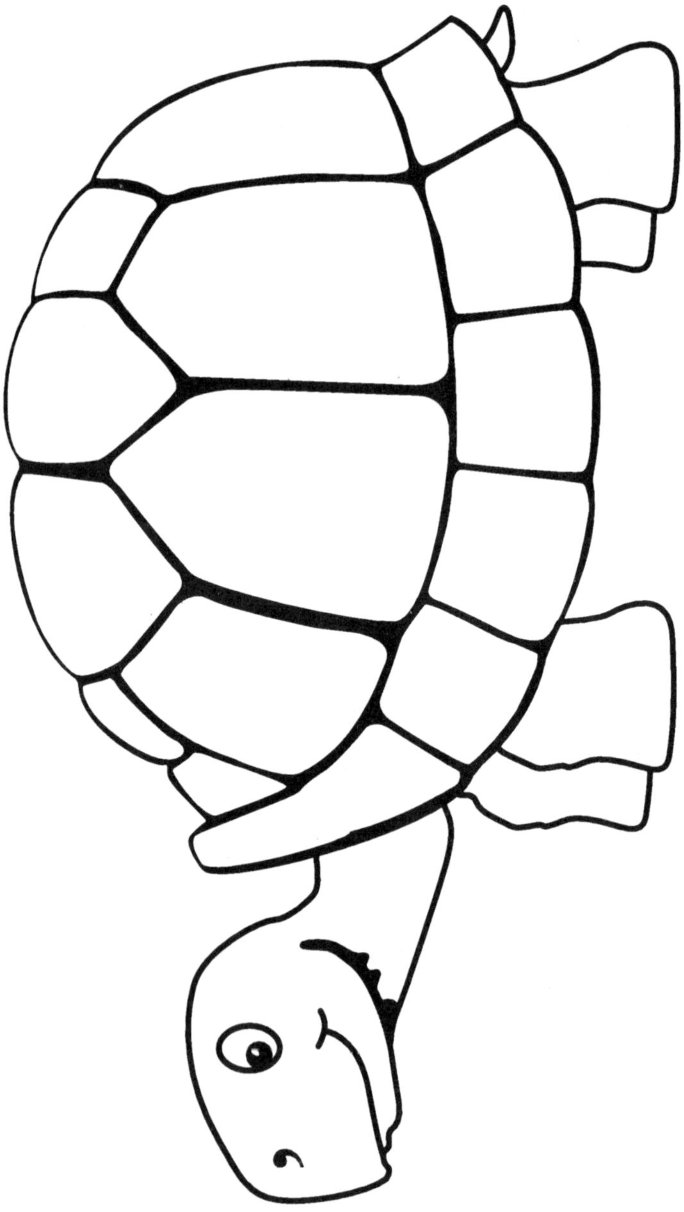

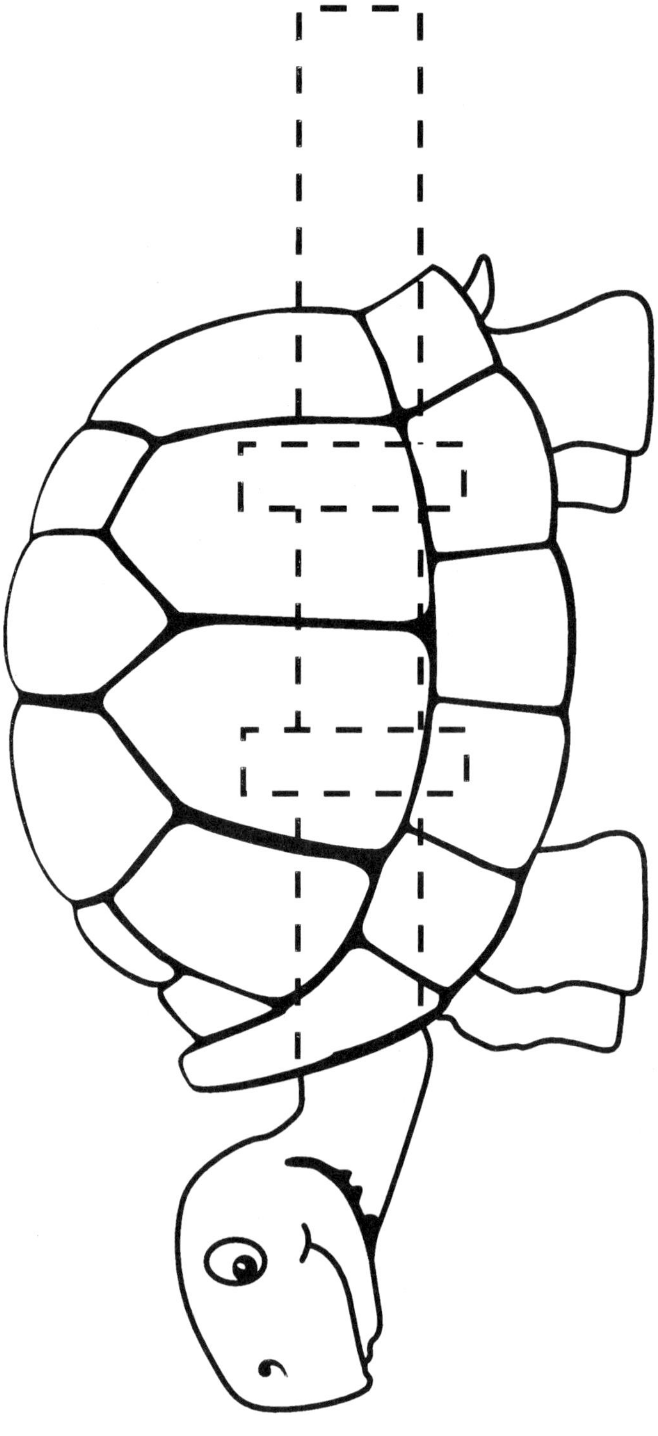

TORTOISE

Make: **A hibernating tortoise**

Any colour A4 activity paper
Brown paper/card
Straw
Black pen/crayon
Scissors
Glue
Card for template

1. The A4 paper is the tortoise's box. Cut a slit, as illustrated, big enough for the tortoise to slide through.

2. Draw circles using dots for the children to join up or they can draw circles themselves to represent holes in the box.

3. Put a small amount of glue in the 'holes' and along the outside of the slit and stick on pieces of straw to make it look as if straw is sticking out of the box. Let the children choose a name for the tortoise and write it on the side of the 'box' eg Tommy's box.

4. Make a template of the tortoise and cut out of brown card/paper or photocopy onto card and colour if necessary.

5. Let the children colour the shell and eyes with pen/crayon.

6. Make a crease in the neck so that the tortoise can be tucked in when he goes in the box.

Rhyme:

A tortoise moves slowly,
Close to the ground.
His little feet plodding,
Without any sound.
On his back is his shell,
and he doesn't complain.
For it keeps out all weather -
The snow, frost and rain! JA

Activity: Make a tortoise with a moving head - Cut out a tortoise shell with felt using picture opposite. Cut out the head and long strip as shown. Fix the head by means of 2 vertical strips of card secured at the back of the tortoise with sticky tape enabling the horizontal strip and head to move through and along, so moving the head in and out of the shell.

Talk about: What does a tortoise look like? What does he use his shell for? Has anyone seen a tortoise? Make up a story about a tortoise that goes to sleep in a box for winter.

Place straight edge on fold

RABBIT

Make: **A rabbit mask**

White card
Elastic and needles
Brown and pink crayons
Black pen/crayon
Card for templates
Scissors

1. Make a template of a rabbit mask and cut out of white card or photocopy onto card.

2. Colour the inside of the ears with pink crayon.

3. Colour the rest of the mask brown.

4. Draw on whiskers with crayon or stick on thin strips of black paper or pipe cleaners,

Rhyme:

If a rabbit is wild, he lives in a burrow,
Which goes right under the ground.
But if he's a pet, so as not to get wet,
In a hutch is where he'll be found! JA

Activity: Make a pencil holder. Cut out the rabbit as illustrated. Colour it in. Fix a cardboard roll tube to the back. Place onto a circle of card to make a base. The tube can be covered with paper/wallpaper etc before sticking to the rabbit. The template could be a back or front view of a rabbit.

Talk about:

Has anyone got a pet rabbit?
What are their names?
What do rabbits look like?
What are their special features?
How do they move?
What do they eat?
Where do they live?

SQUIRREL

Make: **A squirrel threading card**

Suitably coloured card
Thick brown wool
Needles (blunt ended)
Scissors
Card for template

1. Make a template of the squirrel and cut out a squirrel shape from suitably coloured card for each child. Punch an even number of holes in each shape.

2. Tie the wool firmly between the first two holes on the squirrel so that it won't easily become unthreaded. Knot the wool onto the needle.

3. Let the children thread their own cards.

4. Finish off the wool securely at the end.

Rhyme:

In my garden every day,
2 little squirrels come to play.
They chase each other in the trees,
They hide themselves among the leaves.
But in winter when snow lies deep,
All the squirrels go to sleep. JA

Activity: Make a card template of the squirrel on the opposite page. Let the children draw round it, colour it, cut it out and fix onto a length of green garden cane. The children could then get into pairs and dramatise the rhyme.

Talk about:

Where do squirrels live?
What do they eat?
How do they cope with the winter?

my animal counting book

____

1 monkey

2 lions

3 giraffes

4 elephants

5 snakes

SHAPE

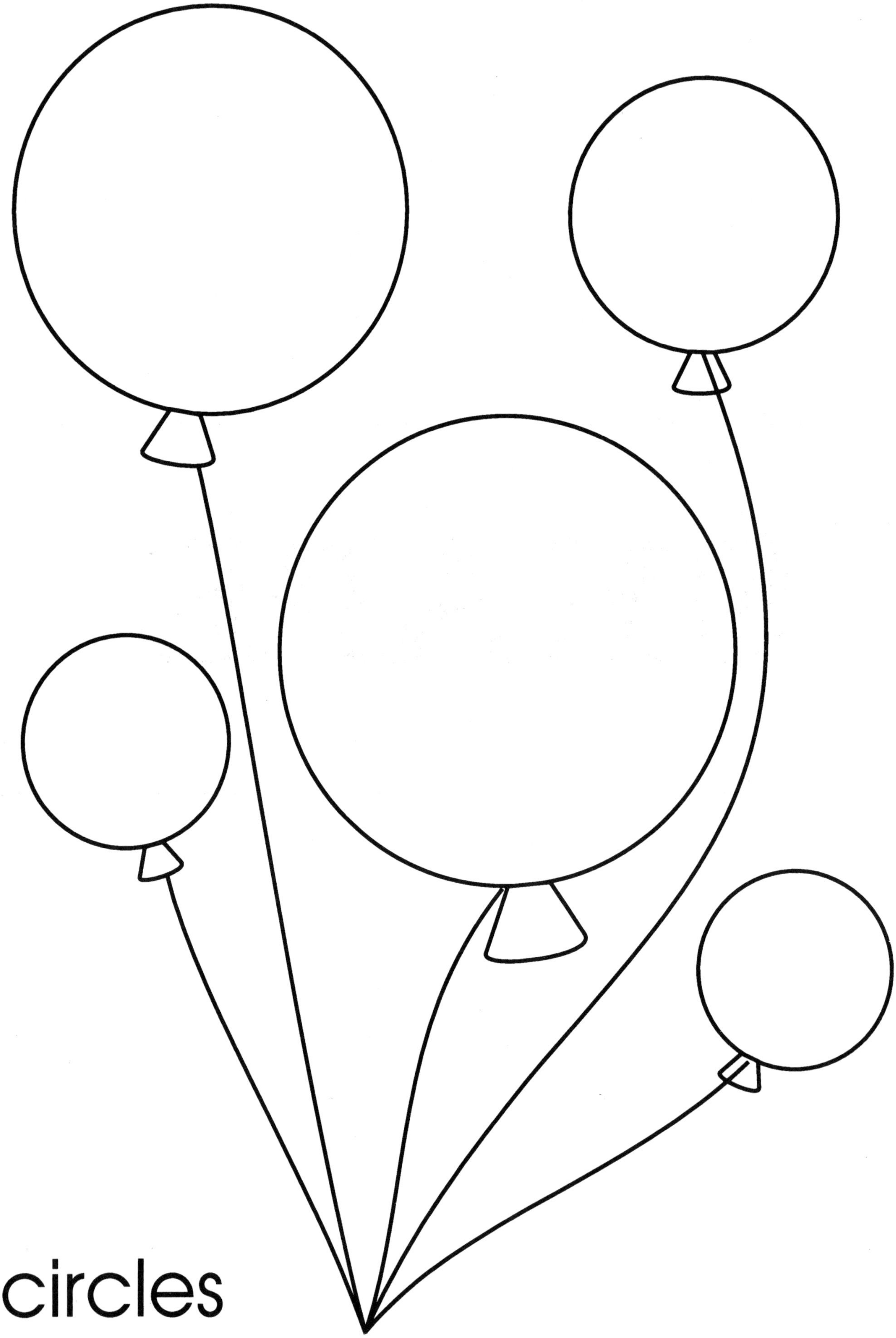

circles

CIRCLE

Make: **A bunch of balloons**

A4 white paper
Card for templates
Coloured paper
Scissors
Glue

1. Photocopy or trace the sheet illustrated opposite for each child.

2. Prepare templates of the different sized circles out of card.

3. According to the age/ability of the children - cut out the circles from the coloured paper or let the children do it so that each child has a set of corresponding circles to the balloons on the sheet.

4. Ask the child to match his set of balloons with those on the sheet.

5. Glue the coloured balloons onto the sheet.

Rhyme:

A circle is round,
Just like a ball.
It has no corners,
or sides at all! JA

Activity: Use as many different objects to print circles with as possible: eg. cotton reels, wheels from toy vehicles, tin lids, beakers, counters, coins, carrot, cucumber etc.

Talk about:

What are the special properties of a circle?
Look around - which things are circular?
Have certain things got to be circular eg wheels?
What would happen if wheels weren't round etc?

Triangle lotto

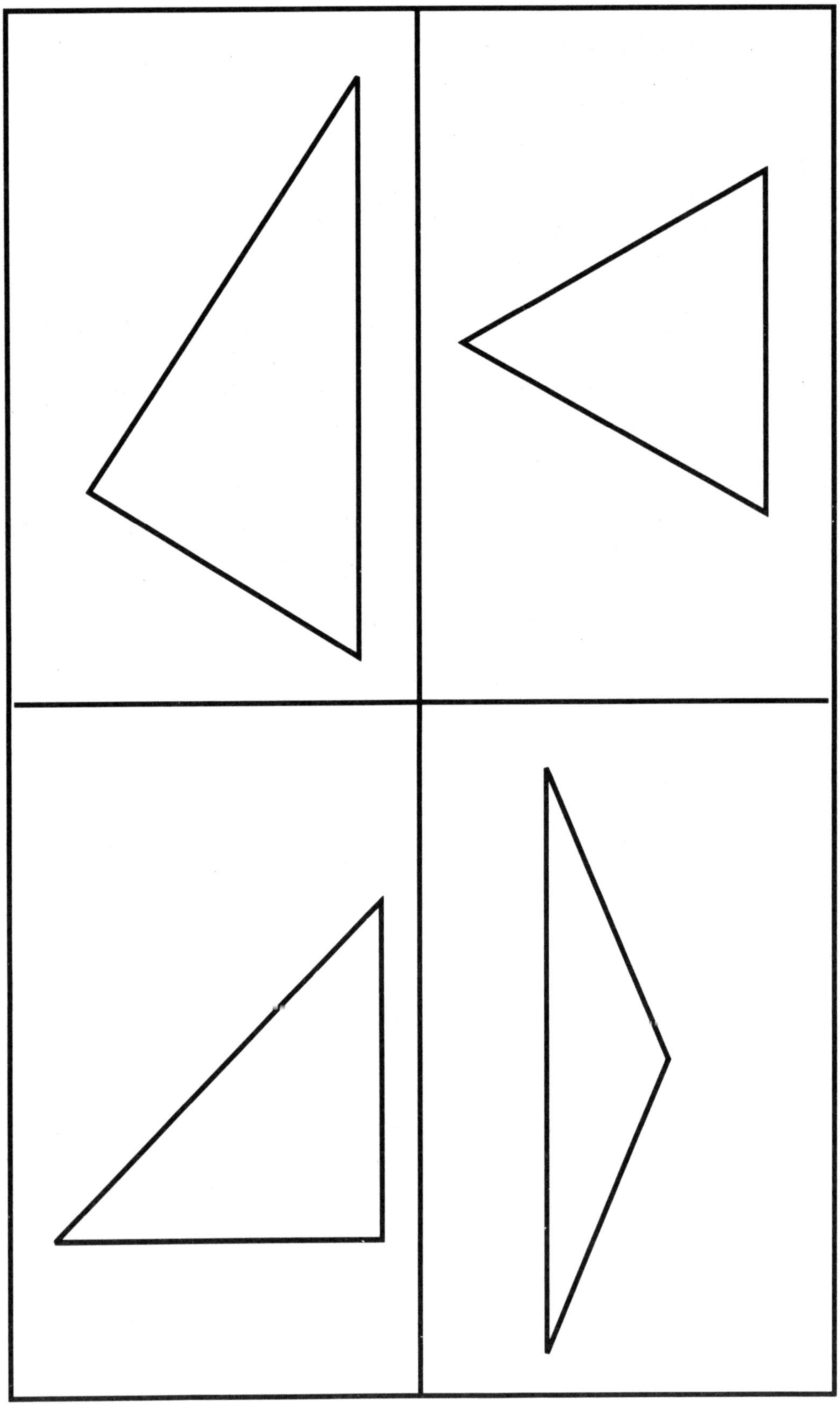

TRIANGLE

Make: **A triangle lotto game**

Crayons/felt pens in red, yellow, green, blue
White A4 card
Scissors

1. Photocopy the sheet opposite 8 times onto white card.

2. Using 4 of the cards colour all the triangles on one card red, on another all yellow, on another all green and another all blue.

3. Cut these into 16 individual lotto cards.

4. On the other 4 photcopied cards, colour one triangle red, one yellow, one green, one blue but different combinations on each card.

5. When play commences make sure that each player has his card the same way round to avoid confusion.

6. The game can be played with 1 - 4 players plus an adult holding up the lotto cards one at a time or alternatively the children can take it in turns to pick up a card from the pack.

Rhyme: How many corners can you see?
The same as the edges 1, 2, 3! JA

Activity: Using ready cut out gummed triangles make a picture of a yacht sailing on the sea.
See earlier activity - a hat with 3 corners.

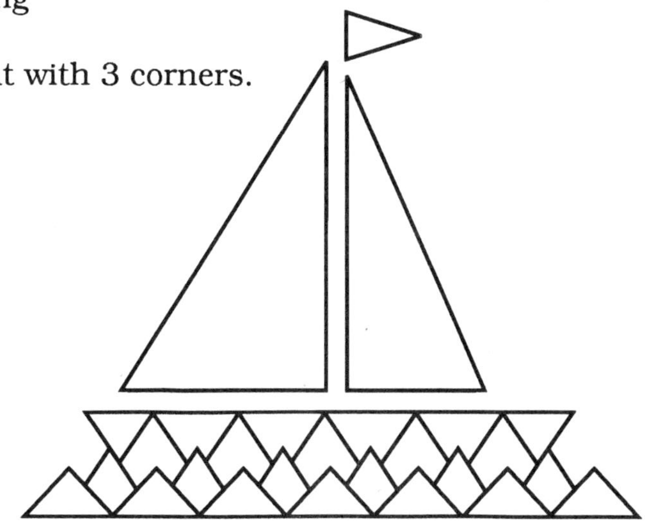

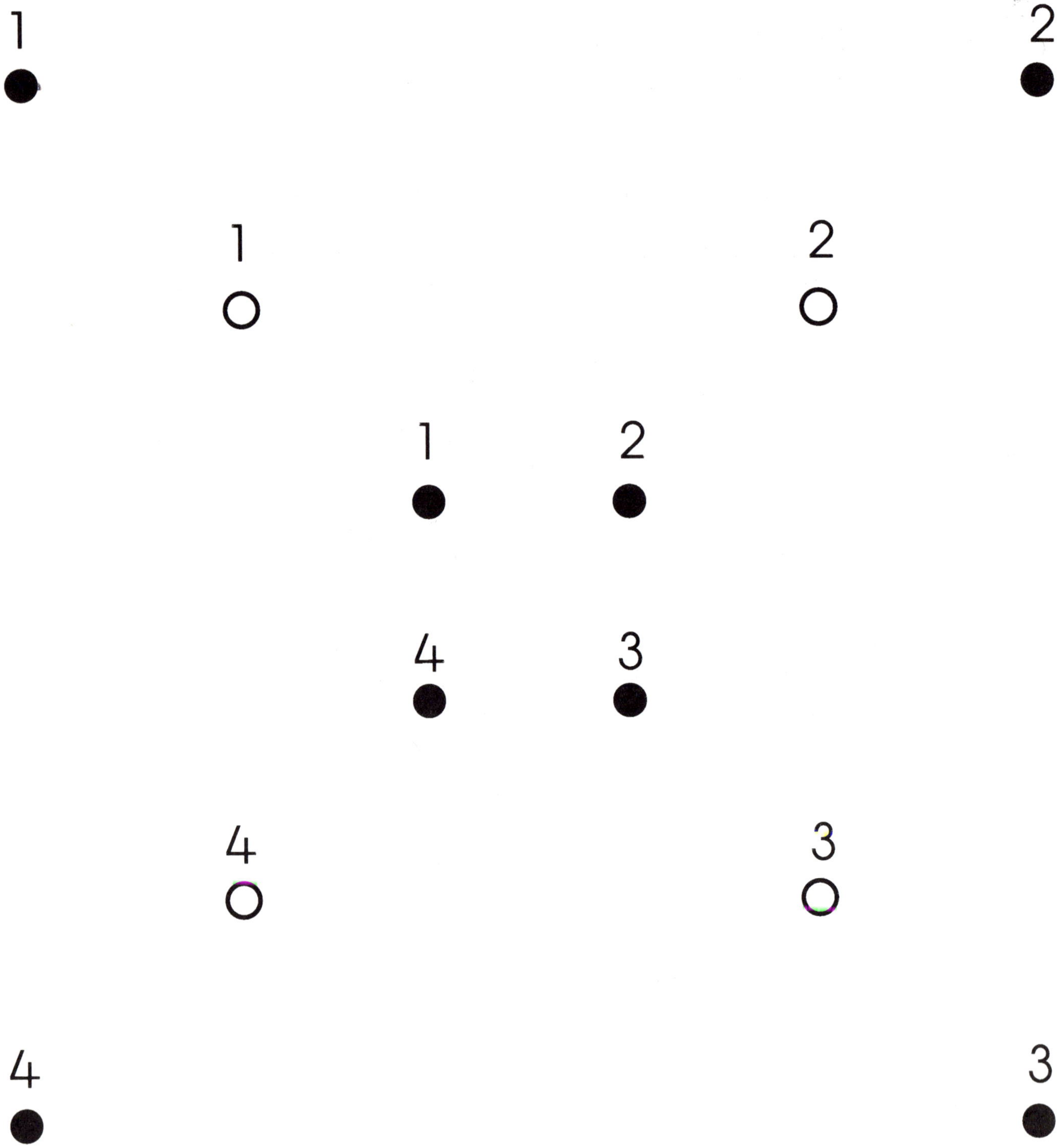

squares

SQUARE

Make: **Dot to dot squares**

A4 white paper
Pencils
Rulers (according to age/ability of children)

1. Photocopy sheet opposite, a copy per child.

2. Join the dots to make the square but first trace round the shapes with the fingers and talk about how many sides each square has.

This activity can also be done with triangles and rectangles.

Rhyme:

Join up the dots
and what have you there?
A circle? A triangle?
No, it's a square! JA

Activity: Cut out a square from stiff card and punch an even number of holes in it around the 4 sides. Use is as a threading card. When completed, write in the middle of the square
- 'square' or 'my square' or if it is going on display 'Peter's square', thus enabling the children to become familiar with the written word as well as the actual shape.

Talk about:

How many sides has a square?
How many corners? If we stand a square on one of its corners what name do we give to that shape?
Can you see any squares around us?
What is a cube?
Look at a cube and look for examples around us.

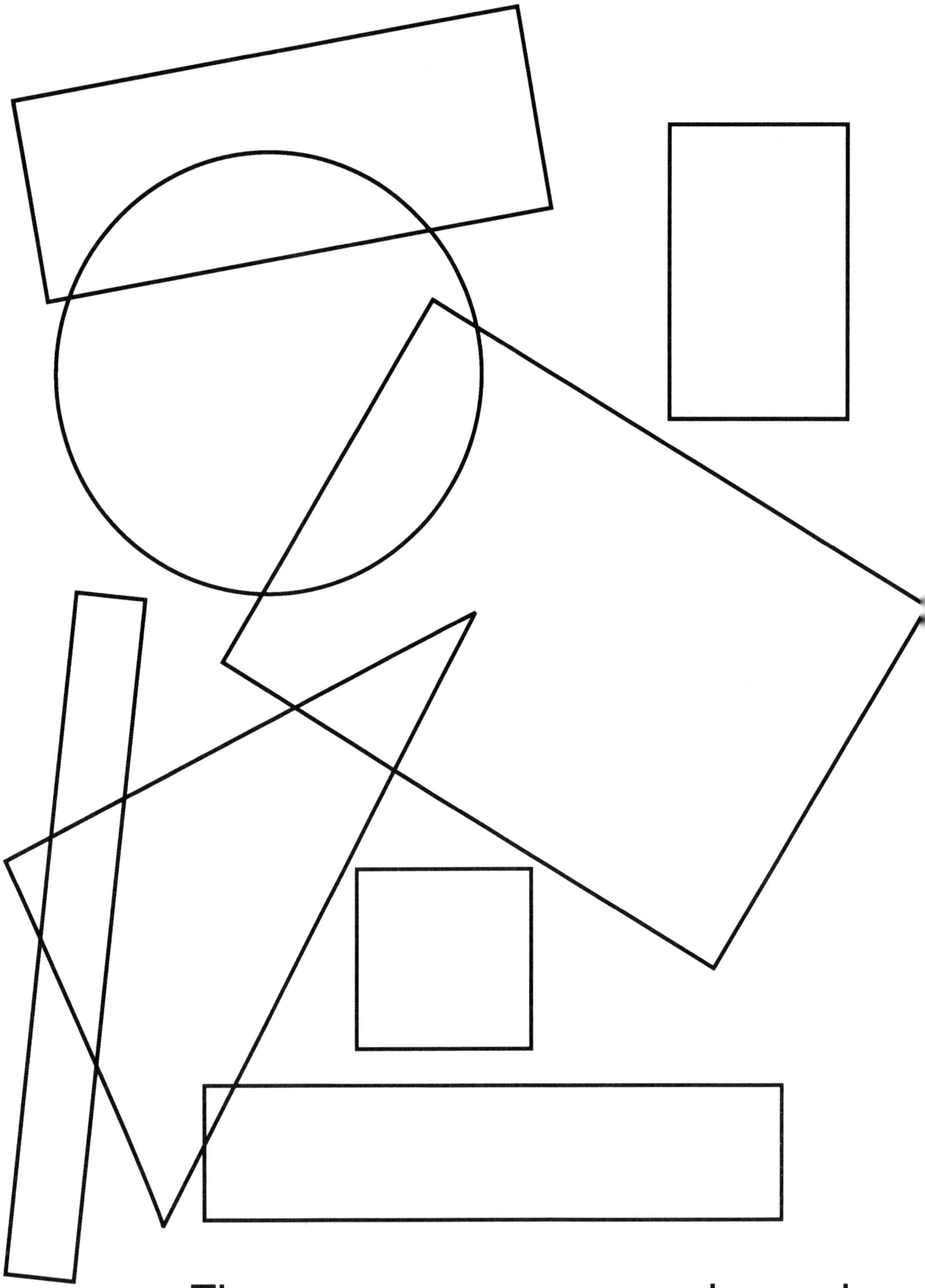

There are ____ rectangles

RECTANGLE

Make: **Look out for rectangles**

A4 white paper
Crayons

1. Photocopy the sheet opposite, a copy per child,

2. Using the fingers, trace round each shape in turn to identify them.

3. Find the rectangles, colour them.

4. Fill in the number on the sheet.

Rhyme:

A door, a book, a window frame,
The shape we call them is the same
- a rectangle! JA

Activity:

Look at a brick wall or a picture of a wall and talk about how the bricks are placed to stop the wall from falling over. Use wooden bricks as printing blocks to print a wall. This could be used in conjunction with other shapes to make a shape picture/frieze/collage etc.

Talk about:

How many sides has a rectangle?
How many corners has a rectangle?
Why is a rectangle diferent from a square?
Look at cuboids.

colour: the squares □ red
the circles ○ yellow
the rectangles ▭ blue
the triangles △ green

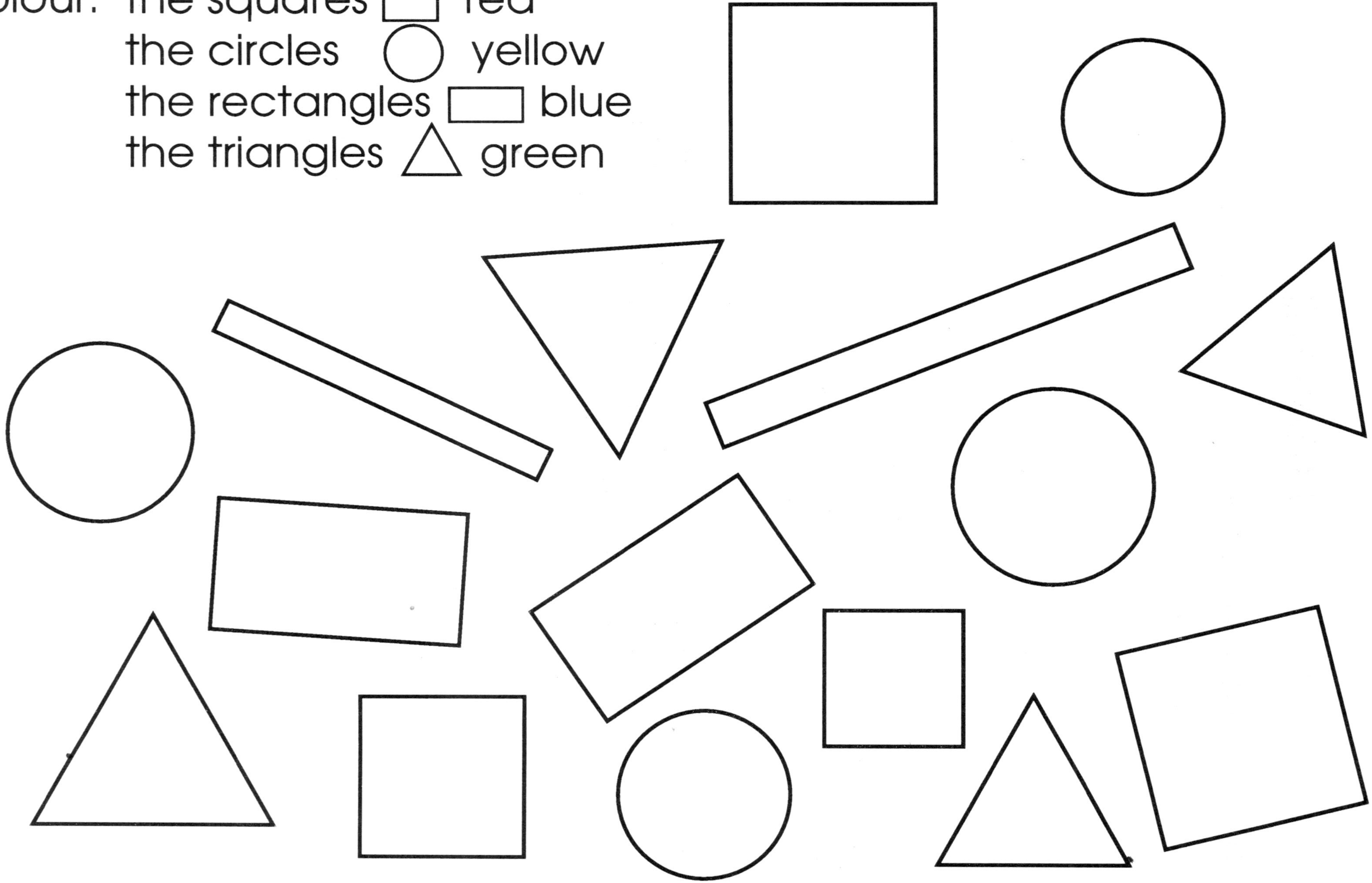

ALL SHAPES

Make: **Have you remembered which shapes are which?**

A4 white paper
Crayons, red, yellow, blue, green

1. Photocopy the sheet opposite, a copy for each child.
2. Read the instructions with the child and colour in the key accordingly.
3. Let the child find the shapes - one shape at a time and colour them in.
4. The shapes that are the same could be joined together in the appropriate colour.

Rhyme:

Shapes are all around us,
Shapes are everywhere.
Shapes are in a cupboard,
Shapes are on my chair.

Shapes are on the ceiling,
Shapes are on the floor.
Shapes are in the window,
Shapes are on the door. JA

Activity: Make a book of shapes. Photocopy the sheets as shown. Cut them in half and staple together to make a book. Complete a page at a time as each shape is introduced.

Talk about: Put 4 large hoops on the floor or draw 4 large circles with chalk. Label each one: Circles, triangles, squares, rectangles. Let the children find examples of the shape and put the objects into the right circle. Talk about them.

my book about shapes

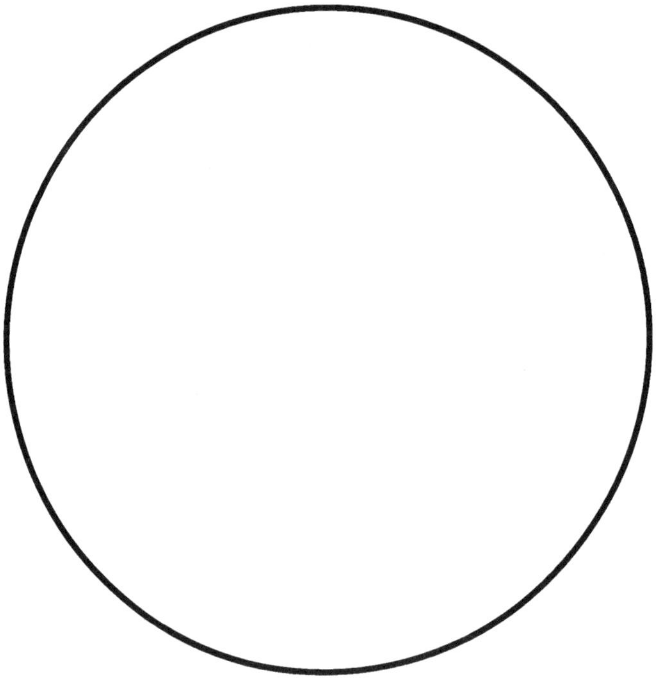

a yellow circle

a red square

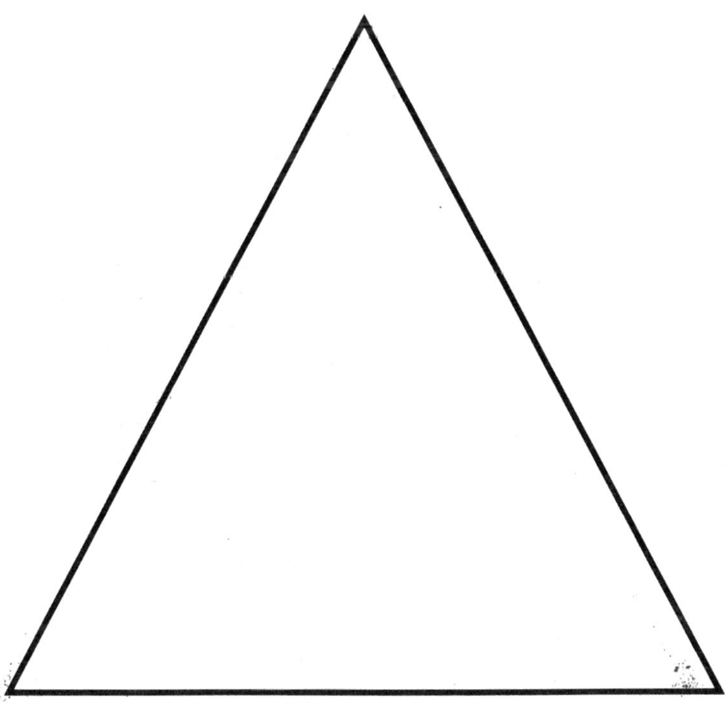

a green triangle

a blue rectangle

match the shapes

THE SHAPE TEAM

Make: **Cindy Circle** **Tina Triangle**
Sam Square **Rob Rectangle**

The Shape Team can be used in a variety of ways including:-

1. Photocopy the sheets and use for colouring and counting eg. How many circles can you count on Cindy Circle?

2. As above, but staple the sheets together to make a book eg. 'My book about shapes' or 'The Shape Team'.

3. Cut out the body parts from card and make the arms and legs with string. Fix together with glue or sticky tape and thread a length of cotton from the top so the characters can be used as puppets or as mobiles.

4. As above but stick the parts onto paper for the child to form into the characters as illustrated.

5. Look at each character separately. Provide the child with the appropriate Shapes but in different sizes and let him create his own shape character plus its name.

6. Try and make the characters from solid shapes eg. cereal boxes, chocolate boxes, polystyrene shapes etc.

7. Invent further members of the team using other shapes eg. oval, star, heart, semi-circle etc.

Cindy Circle

Tina Triangle

Sam Square

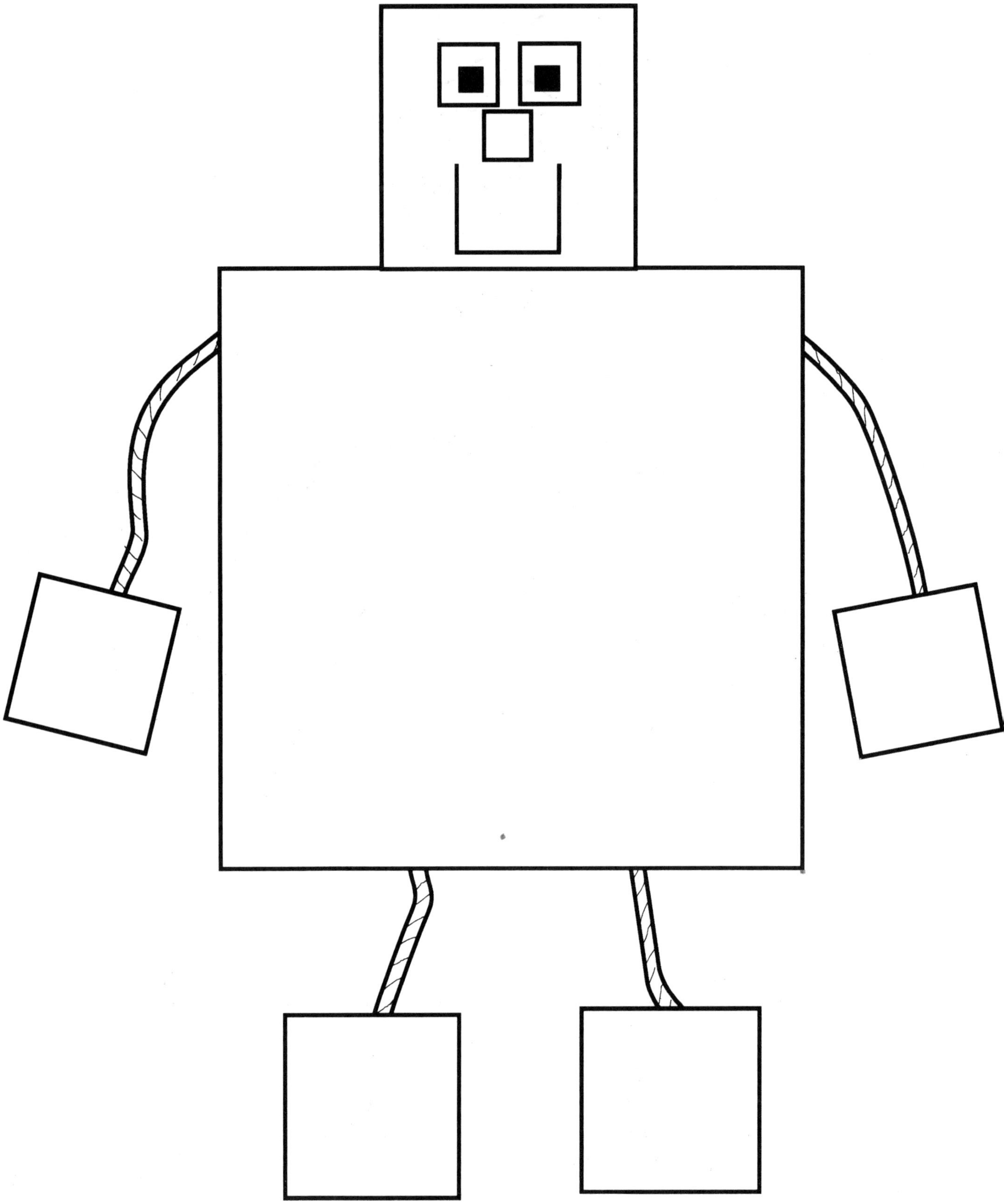

Rob Rectangle

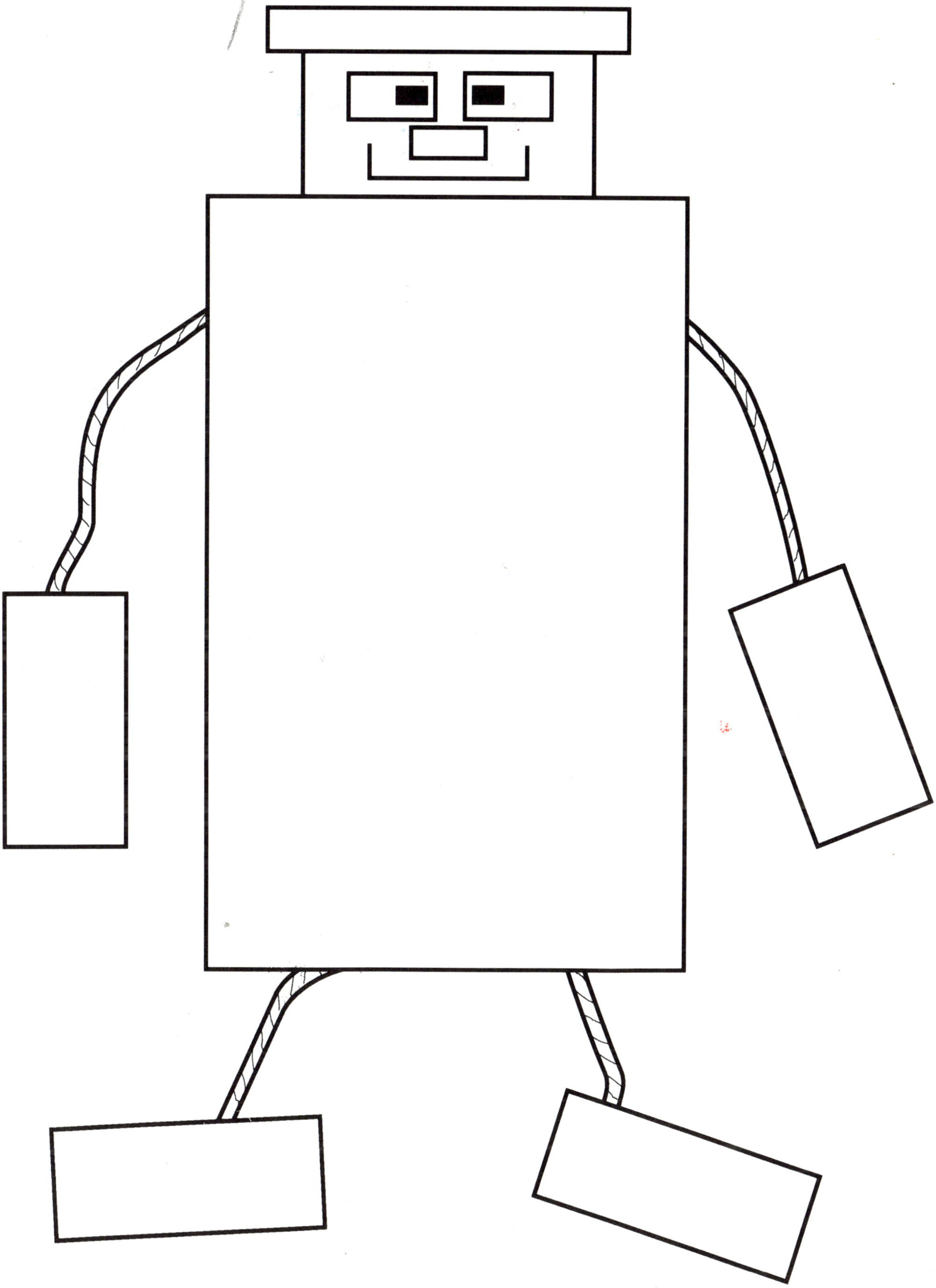

If you have found this book useful, Part I "Practical Topics for the Early Years" can be obtained directly from Topical Resources, PO Box 329, Broughton, Preston PR3 5LT. Telephone 01772 863158.

Topical Resources provide a range of materials for nursery / primary schools. A catalogue can be obtained from the above address.